WHAT SHOULD THIS BOOK BEE ABOUT?

Colee Regelman

Author League
Inspire critical thinking, creativity, collaboration, and communication
Books@AuthorLeague.com

I want to write a book, but I don't know what it should bee about!

Should it be about a bee?

Or maybe a butterfly?

What about a car?

I have an idea!
Let's use all three—
because I'm three!

The bee and the butterfly fly into a car.
The windows are shiny and bright.
The sun makes it feel like they are outside!

Uh oh! They are stuck inside the car.
They ask, "Where are we going?"

The butterfly is scared.
"Don't worry," says the bee.
"I'll help us find the way."

Suddenly, the car door opens. Out they fly.
Buzz, buzz! Flutter, flutter!
"Let's go to my hive for a sweet surprise!"
says the bee.

They reach the hive and taste the honey.
It is sweet, sticky, and oh so yummy!

Everything is just right.

You can write your own story too.
Just bee you!

Author League

Published by Author League, ISBN: 978-1-63971-756-9, Photo Attributions: CanvaPro, Copyright © 2024 Author League, All rights reserved. No part of this publication may be reproduced or utilized in any form or by any means without written permission from the publisher.

www.ingramcontent.com/pod-product-compliance
Lightning Source LLC
Chambersburg PA
CBHW041525070526
44585CB00002B/87